POWERED UP!

A STEM Approach to Energy Sources

SOLAR PANELS

Harnessing the Power of the Sun

JADE ZORA SCIBILIA

PowerKiDS
press

New York

Published in 2018 by The Rosen Publishing Group, Inc.
29 East 21st Street, New York, NY 10010

First Edition

Editor: Melissa Raé Shofner
Book Design: Tanya Dellaccio

Photo Credits: Cover VioNet/Shutterstock.com; p. 4 (Bangkok) charnsitr/ Shutterstock.com; p. 4 (New York City) blvdone/Shutterstock.com; pp. 5, 17 (left) ESA/ Handout/Getty Images Publicity/Getty Images; p. 7 (house) esbobeldijk/ Shutterstock.com; pp. 7 (middle left), 13 Praethip Docekalova/Shutterstock.com; p. 7 (middle right) pedrosala/Shutterstock.com; p. 7 (smartphone with solar charger) Dmitry Galaganov/Shutterstock.com; p. 9 (top) Cholpan/Shutterstock.com; p. 9 (bottom) Varlamova Lydmila/Shutterstock.com; p. 10 (left) yoshi0511/Shutterstock.com; p. 10 (right) Thunayaporn Arunsmith/Shutterstock.com; p. 11 hans engbers/Shutterstock.com; p. 15 Ernesto r. Ageitos/Moment/Getty Images; p. 16 Stocktrek Images/Getty Images; p. 17 (right) NASA/Handout/Getty Images News/Getty Images; p. 19 (top) Frederic Stevens/Getty Images News/Getty Images; p. 19 (bottom) CHARLY TRIBALLEAU/AFP/ Getty Images; p. 20 (left) VALERIE GACHE/AFP/Getty Images; p. 20 (right) Handout/ Getty Images News/Getty Images; p. 21 P A Thompson/Corbis Documentary/ Getty Images; p. 22 Diyana Dimitrova/Shutterstock.com.

Cataloging-in-Publication Data

Names: Scibilia, Jade Zora.
Title: Solar panels: harnessing the power of the sun / Jade Zora Scibilia.
Description: New York : PowerKids Press, 2018. | Series: Powered up! a STEM approach to energy sources | Includes index.
Identifiers: ISBN 9781538328545 (pbk.) | ISBN 9781508164258 (library bound) | ISBN 9781538328606 (6 pack)
Subjects: LCSH: Solar energy–Juvenile literature. | Solar cells–Juvenile literature.
Classification: LCC TJ810.3 S35 2018 | DDC 621.47–dc23

Manufactured in China

CPSIA Compliance Information: Batch #BW18PK For Further Information contact Rosen Publishing, New York, New York at 1-800-237-9932

CONTENTS

MORE PEOPLE, MORE POWER

Today, there are about 7.4 billion people on Earth. It takes a lot of energy to meet the population's power needs. We burn **fossil fuels** to power our homes and cars, but these fuels won't last forever. They also create a lot of pollution, which is harmful for the **environment**.

Luckily, we can get power from other energy sources that are cleaner, safer, and sustainable, which means they'll last a long time. In fact, Earth spins around one of the best sources of renewable energy—the sun.

WE USE SO MUCH ELECTRICITY THAT OUR STREETLIGHTS CAN BE SEEN FROM OUTER SPACE. THIS PHOTOGRAPH OF LONDON, ENGLAND, WAS TAKEN FROM THE INTERNATIONAL SPACE STATION (ISS) AND CLEARLY SHOWS THE CITY BLOCKS.

SUPERCHARGED!

Your **ecological** footprint is a measurement of how much energy you use and your impact, or effect, on the environment. If every person lived like the average American, we'd need nearly four Earths to meet the needs of the current population!

WHAT ARE SOLAR PANELS?

The sun produces a huge amount of **electromagnetic** energy, which travels to Earth in the form of sunlight. We can put this energy to work using solar panels.

Solar panels are devices that absorb, or take in, energy from the sun and change it into electricity. They work like batteries, which are objects that store energy. Electricity is the form of energy you're probably most familiar with—you use it every day when you turn on a light, ride in a car, or use a computer.

SUPERCHARGED!

Plants are solar powered, too! They use their leaves to absorb energy from the sun, then convert, or change, it into food using **photosynthesis**.

LARGE SOLAR PANELS CAN BE PLACED ON TOP OF BUILDINGS OR ARRANGED IN FIELDS CALLED SOLAR FARMS OR SOLAR PARKS. VERY SMALL SOLAR PANELS CAN BE USED WITH HANDHELD DEVICES SUCH AS CELL PHONES.

HOW SOLAR PANELS WORK

During the daytime, the sun shines on the surface of a solar panel. The solar panel converts the energy from the sun into electricity using an inverter. Extra energy can be stored in a battery or sent back to the power company for later use. Extra energy can be used at other times, such as when the sun isn't shining or when more power is needed to run electronic devices.

Solar panels should be positioned to face the sun so they can absorb as much sunlight—and make as much electricity—as possible.

SUPERCHARGED!

The first person to study the possibility of using solar panels was Antoine-César Becquerel in 1839. An engineer named Russell Ohl invented modern solar panels in 1941.

INVERTER ON THE BACK OF A SOLAR PANEL

SOLAR PANELS CAN PROVIDE POWER FOR A HOUSE BY CONVERTING SUNLIGHT INTO ELECTRICITY. FIRST, THE PANELS ABSORB SUNLIGHT. NEXT, AN INVERTER CONVERTS THE SUN'S ENERGY INTO A USABLE FORM OF ELECTRICITY. A METER KEEPS TRACK OF HOW MUCH ELECTRICITY IS BEING USED. EXTRA ELECTRICITY MAY BE STORED IN A BATTERY FOR LATER USE.

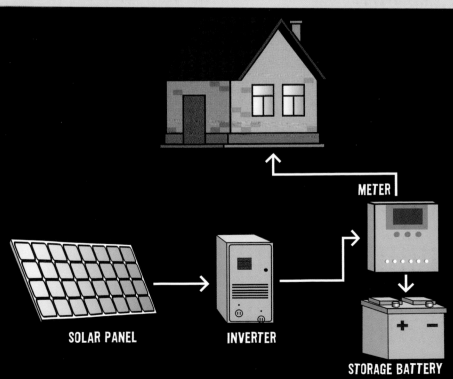

METER

SOLAR PANEL

INVERTER

STORAGE BATTERY

WHY GO SOLAR?

There are many benefits to using solar panels. For one, they're better for the planet than fossil fuels because they don't create **greenhouse gases**. Solar panels may also be placed on existing structures without harming the surrounding environment.

Solar energy is a sustainable source of clean energy. It reduces our dependence on fossil fuels. It also creates jobs. Solar panels need to be built, put into place, and kept in working order. Working with solar energy is safer than working with fossil fuels and **nuclear** energy.

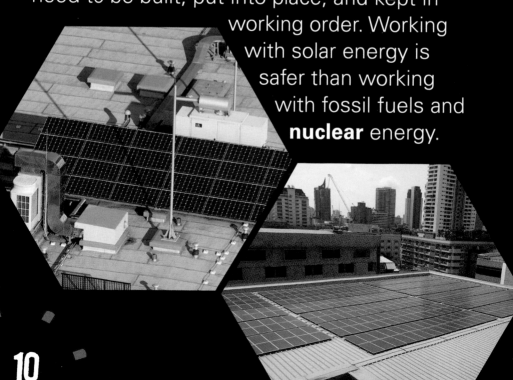

SOLAR PANELS IN NEW OLDENZAAL, NETHERLANDS, ARE MAKING USE OF OTHERWISE WASTED SPACE—THE SIDE OF AN OFFICE BUILDING. THEY'RE ANGLED AND ARRANGED SO THEY ABSORB THE MOST SUNLIGHT POSSIBLE.

SUPERCHARGED!

Greenhouse gases include carbon dioxide, methane, water vapor, ozone, and others. These harmful gases are making Earth's temperature rise, which is called global warming.

NOTHING'S PERFECT

Solar panels aren't perfect. However, there aren't many downsides to using them. Perhaps the most apparent issue is that solar power can't be generated, or created, at night. It's also harder to produce solar power on cloudy days.

Building solar panels creates pollution and waste. Once they're set up, the panels need to be kept clean so they stay in proper working order. Another downside is that land must be cleared to make space for a solar farm, which may harm local wildlife.

SUPERCHARGED!

Even the most **efficient** solar panels are able to convert only about 20 percent of sunlight to electricity. If solar panels become dirty, this amount is reduced even more.

COMPARE THE SIZE OF THIS SOLAR FARM TO THE SIZE OF NEARBY HOMES.

13

USING THE POWER OF THE SUN

Solar power can be used in many ways. With solar panels, we're able to use energy from the sun to power anything that requires electricity, including cell phones, flashlights, buildings, homes, and cars.

As fossil fuels become more expensive and harder to find, people will look for cheaper and cleaner sources of energy. Solar-panel **technology** will continue to improve over time. Solar panels will likely become smaller and more efficient in the coming years.

SUPERCHARGED!

The first electric automobile was built in the 1830s, but it was very basic. Today, cars that run on electricity are becoming more and more common.

BATTERIES FOR SOME ELECTRIC CARS MAY BE
CHARGED AT SOLAR-POWERED CHARGING STATIONS.

IN OUTER SPACE

Scientists have built a lab in outer space called the International Space Station. Astronauts and scientists from over a dozen countries have lived and worked on the ISS.

Solar panels are sometimes used to supply power to man-made objects in space. **Satellites** and the International Space Station all operate on electricity generated using solar panels. Without solar panels, scientists would have a harder time studying things beyond Earth, and we'd have big gaps in our knowledge and understanding of outer space.

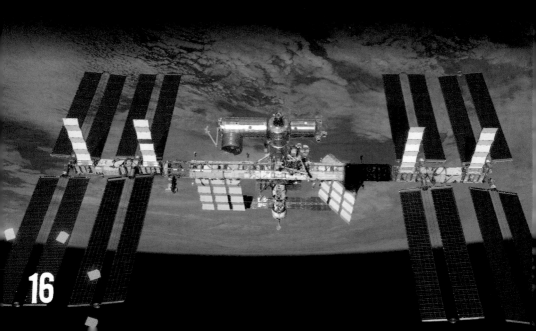

SPACEX DRAGON SPACECRAFT WITH SOLAR PANELS

HUBBLE SPACE TELESCOPE WITH SOLAR PANELS

SUPERCHARGED!

Scientists on the ISS conduct experiments that help them learn more about outer space, the weather, and life on Earth.

THE INTERNATIONAL SPACE STATION'S SOLAR PANELS ARE HUGE. THEY COVER ABOUT 27,000 SQUARE FEET (2,508.4 SQ M), WHICH IS EQUAL TO MORE THAN HALF A FOOTBALL FIELD!

THE FUTURE OF SOLAR ENERGY

When it comes to solar panels, the opportunities are endless! The transportation, computing, and space industries are all looking into ways to use solar panels.

Since solar panels convert the sun's energy into electricity, anything that uses electricity can be powered by the sun. However, solar-energy technology doesn't stop there. Any sort of flat surface—such as a highway, sidewalk, or a parking lot—may be used for solar panels to collect energy. This solar energy can then be converted to electricity.

SUPERCHARGED!

There are 4.12 million miles (6,630,497.3 km) of roads in the United States. Imagine how much renewable, sustainable energy could be generated if even a small percentage of these surfaces were converted to solar roads!

FRANCE'S FIRST SOLAR ROAD WAS OPENED IN THE VILLAGE OF TOUROUVRE AU PERCHE ON DECEMBER 22, 2016. ON A SMALL SCALE, SOLAR ROADS COULD POWER ROAD SIGNS AND STREETLIGHTS. ON A LARGE SCALE, THEY COULD POWER WHOLE TOWNS!

WHAT CAN YOU DO?

Every person can make a difference in the future of our planet. Calculate your family's ecological footprint, then think about ways to reduce your energy usage. Switching your home to solar power would be a big step to a more sustainable, cleaner, and safer energy environment.

There are small steps you can take, too. Turn off lights when you leave a room, use power strips, unplug electronics when not in use, or use a clothesline to dry your clothes. There are lots of ways to make a difference!

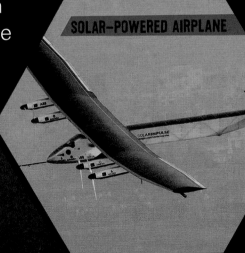
SOLAR-POWERED AIRPLANE

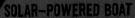
SOLAR-POWERED BOAT

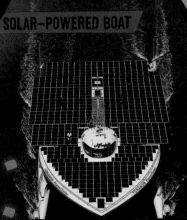

IN EARLY 2016, HOUSTON, TEXAS, BEGAN USING 276 NEW SOLAR-POWERED PARKING METERS. THESE METERS WORK FASTER AND HAVE LONGER-LASTING BATTERIES THAN THOSE THAT AREN'T POWERED BY THE SUN.

SUPERCHARGED!

Scientists and engineers are coming up with new ways to power our planet and use less energy every day. Do you have any ideas about how to improve energy usage? Try thinking outside the box!

THE POWER OF THE SUN

Solar energy is renewable and sustainable. It's also cleaner and safer than using fossil fuels. There aren't many downsides to using solar energy, and engineers are improving the technology every day.

As fossil fuels are used up, solar panels will likely become more common and more efficient. Already, we're seeing new ways to use solar energy in cars, roads, and handheld devices. As more people learn about the benefits of solar energy, the more it will be used and the more it will be improved.

GLOSSARY

ecological: Relating to the way living things are linked with each other and with Earth.

efficient: Capable of producing desired results without wasting materials, time, or energy.

electromagnetic: Relating to the magnetic field that's produced by a current of electricity.

engineer: Someone who uses math and science to do useful things, such as planning and building machines.

environment: The conditions that surround a living thing and affect the way it lives.

fossil fuel: A fuel—such as coal, oil, or natural gas—that is formed in the earth from dead plants or animals.

greenhouse gases: Gases in the atmosphere that trap energy from the sun.

nuclear: Having to do with the power created by splitting atoms, the smallest bits of matter.

photosynthesis: The way in which green plants make their own food from sunlight, water, and a gas called carbon dioxide.

satellite: A spacecraft placed in orbit around Earth, a moon, or a planet to collect information or for communication.

technology: A method that uses science to solve problems and the tools used to solve those problems.

INDEX

WEBSITES